SANDTIME HAPPINESS: A SWEET FANTASY.

Legal & Disclaimer

The information contained in this book and its contents is not designed to replace or take the place of any form of medical or professional advice; and is not meant to replace the need for independent medical, financial, legal or other professional advice or services, as may be required. The content and information in this book has been provided for educational and entertainment purposes only.

The content and information contained in this book has been compiled from sources deemed reliable, and it is accurate to the best of the Author's knowledge, information and belief. However, the Author cannot guarantee its accuracy and validity and cannot be held liable for any errors and/or omissions. Further, changes are periodically made to this book as and when needed. Where appropriate and/or necessary, you must consult a professional (including but not limited to your doctor, attorney, financial advisor or such other professional advisor) before using any of the suggested remedies, techniques, or information in this book.

Upon using the contents and information contained in this book, you agree to hold harmless the Author from and against any damages, costs, and expenses, including any legal fees potentially resulting from the application of any of the information provided by this book. This disclaimer applies to any loss, damages or injury caused by the use and application, whether directly or indirectly, of any advice or information presented, whether for

breach of contract, tort, negligence, personal injury, criminal intent, or under any other cause of action.

You agree to accept all risks of using the information presented inside this book.

You agree that by continuing to read this book, where appropriate and/or necessary, you shall consult a professional (including but not limited to your doctor, attorney, or financial advisor or such other advisor as needed) before using any of the suggested remedies, techniques, or information in this book.

CHAPTER ONE

Desert and Mountain

As Tarlos died, he did not think of his brother, and he did not think of his mother or father. He did not think about his toddling son, as he failed to think of the woman had had given his son life. Part of his mind searched for their faces, but he did not see them. He lay in the dirt with a spear through his chest, neck broken, his thick warm blood pooling around him. Laughter was fresh in his ears, and he did not think of any one specific person. Instead, he thought about a tooth. A single, lone tooth stood out in the back of his mind.

The air around him was dry, and the day was dusty and hot. He had been sweating not five minutes earlier as he battled the foe that would cause his end—but now the air seemed cool, and he did not turn his gaze from upon the sight of his blood that now lied circling his body. He was angry and confused that this was how it would end for him, but at least he was comfortable. His eyes closed, and the darkness came, and all he could think about was the that one single tooth.

The tooth had once belonged to a cow. By the time Tarlos found it, the cow was nothing more than a bleached skeleton lying in the desert. Small bits of fur clung to the ribs on strips of its now dried leather. Its jaw held frozen in an eerily gaped-open position, and its neck was bent backward as if it was a fragile flower wilted on the hot desert sands. The legs spread beneath it in a sort of running position. The skeleton gave Tarlos the impression that the cow's death was a slow and painful one. It had most likely died of thirst.

The bones reminded Tarlos of his own thirst, as he tipped his water bag to his mouth, using his bent elbow to lift it. He let the water only just past his lips before pulling back. He was not sure how much longer it would take him to reach the mountain, and the hide bag was almost empty. There was no water to be found here.

Tarlos knelt beside the skull and stared into the empty sockets that once held eyes. He narrowed his own eyes. As anger welled up inside him. The skeleton reminded him of Krastos.

He imagined that there was a day when this cow walked around, breathing, letting out bellows in the desert. Its heart beat, its tail swished the flies away, and sweat ran down its back and shoulders. And the next day it was dead.

How seamlessly life leads to death.
The ground was old and dry, and the cow had made an impression in the ground before it decomposed. The rains had come, as they did seldom in the desert, and the dirt softened around the cow. After scavengers ate the flesh and the undesirable bits decomposed, the dirt dried. Now there was a perfect image of a cow in the hard, tan ground.

Tarlos could make out the indentations of individual hairs. He had no way of knowing how long ago the cow had given its last breath over to the heat of the desert, but the image in the ground assured him that it had called this barren place its final resting spot for quite some time.

He shook his head at the cow. So much evidence of what was once life, right before his eyes, and yet it was now over. And did anyone remember this cow? Tarlos doubted it.

The cow's jaw was long and white, lined with thick square teeth that clung to the bone. Some of the teeth had loosened over time, yellowed, or disappeared entirely. Tarlos poked at them, feeling how loose or intact they each were, and one fell freely from the jawbone. It was a larger tooth, oddly shaped for one that belonged to a cow. Instead of flat and smooth for grinding plants, this tooth had a sharp tip, and the tip had been chipped long ago.

Tarlos picked up the chipped tooth with his thumb, and then closed his fist around it just before tossing it in his pocket.

He stood, and he clapped the dirt from his hands. He gave one last look to the bleached white skeleton that was once a living, breathing animal and said, "My condolences."

The desert stretched out behind ~~him~~ and ahead of him, and in every direction where it met with the horizon, merging in the distance with the grey - blue sky. Tarlos had grown up in a sort of desert. Of course, this desert connected to his homeland. But his home had food and water. The desert was cursed and barren. It had not rained since he began his journey, and he had lost track of how long ago that was. He guessed around thirty days.

He carried with him two skins of water. One had been empty for two decades. Each time he thought about taking a drink from the second bag, he forced himself to think about other things. The water must be saved for when he could not continue without it.

Tonight, when I bed down, I'll have another drink.

Shar-shu-ma, Shar's Mountain, rose in the distance. There the air shimmered in the heat and played tricks on the mind. When Tarlos first saw the mountain, he thought it must have been a mirage. But there was no doubt about it, in the last few days the mountain had grown larger and its image had become clearer. He was getting closer.

Tarlos's body, and sometimes he could barely walk at all. He was not used to having to walk such an excruciating distance. Being a Holder, however, this was never a concern for him. He fingered the tooth in his pocket and brought it in front of his face. He was tired, and his mind needed focusing, but he managed to lift the tooth from his palm with a little effort.

The tooth hovered a few inches above his hand, and it wriggled a bit before dropping back into his grip. It seemed so long ago that he was able to do that with his own body; when there were entire days that his feet never touched the ground. When was the last time he had flown? He could not remember. Before Krastos died, surely. Perhaps in the fight against Bawa. Tarlos closed his eyes against a flash of violent memory, and his feet carried him farther.

I miss it. The wind in my eyes, screaming past my ears. Seeing the world so tiny below me.

He dropped the tooth into his pocket and looked ahead to the mountain. It resembled the tooth in a way. What may have once been a triangular peak was now cracked down the middle, creating a V-shape. Every morning for the last several days, Tarlos had watched the sun rise from that V in the peak. It was Shar's doorway into the world of the living from that of the dead country.

Tarlos was envious of those who lived beneath the mountain, in that country from which no man returns. At least they were at rest. At least they did not get thirsty or hungry. Here in the living world, there were only sore feet, sand, and skeletons.

A small dusty whirlwind passed in front of him, and he paused to watch it. It was beautiful in its own odd way, twisting and silent. He saw them sometimes when the days were especially hot and dry. He wondered how many there were in the vast stretches of the desert that he missed every day.

The sun beat down on him as he made one step after another. All the while the mountain in the distance loomed over the desert. He would get to that mountain if it was the last thing he ever did.

As his feet screamed in hot pain, ~~and~~ his thighs cramped and called for rest, Tarlos thought about what awaited him if he could only make it through the Tunnel of the Sun and the dead country beyond.

As the day went on, Tarlos forgot about his promise to save his water for emergencies. He touched his lips to the water twice more and made a silent prayer that there would be water on the mountain.

Why would there be? The mountain belongs to the gods, and the gods don't drink water.
He hoped for it nevertheless. Hope was all he had, other than his ragged clothes and a nearly empty bag of water.

And a tooth.
He must not forget his tooth.

He rested during the hottest part of the day when Shar was the highest, and he pushed as far as he could until the sun set behind him and the desert turned a dark shade of purple. Above, the stars blinked, and they watched him.

When the day ended, Tarlos did not bother to build a fire. There was nothing here to burn anyway. He slept in the open and chilly desert air with his bent arm as a pillow and the sky as his blanket.

The last three miles were the most difficult. He lost track of the time he had spent in the desert so far, but he felt every step of that last stretch to the mountain. His water bags had dried completely the day before, and his mouth felt like dry cotton. He tried to swallow, but there was no saliva in his parched mouth and he gagged on his tongue. The beginnings of sores dotted the inside of his mouth, behind his lips and in his cheeks.

It had been three days since the cow. He gripped the tooth in his pocket and pressed on.

The mountain was now taller than he had imagined it was, and it stood over him in an angry brooding way. *How dare you come to me,* it seemed to say. Tarlos craned his neck and looked at the peak: two points that cut the sky above. The sun rose from between those points, and it came from the dead country. The sight made him dizzy, and he stumbled backwards. For a moment his loss of balance brought back a memory, and he slapped his hands to the sides of his face until Krastos's frown left his mind.

You're here, came the voice of his twin brother. *Now what?*

"Be quiet, you're dead," Tarlos said. His voice was dry and cracked, and he did not recognize it as his own.

As the Foothills rose against the mountain, and the brittle grass grew on the foothills. The area around the mountain was a strange island in this ocean of sand, and the off-yellow of the prickly grass was stark against the monotone tan of the desert that surrounded it. The mountain grew lighter as the foothills grew rockier until far above the rock was white as bone. It seemed like an alien thing, a lone mountain in the middle of nowhere, but Tarlos did not linger. There was grass here, brittle and yellow though it was, and that meant one thing.

He heard the trickle and smelled the water before he saw it. The sound and scent woke his exhausted and dehydrated mind, he then jumped to search for it.

A dry crack in the earth ran down the foothills from the mountain, and thicker bunches of the brittle grass grew along the sides of the crack. Tarlos crouched low to it and placed his hands in the dirt.

It was dry and cool. There must be water just beneath the surface. He could hear the trickle, but he could not see it. He stood, not bothering to dust his legs off and clap the dirt from his hands. His mouth gaped, and he did not notice it. His tongue was a dry sponge in his mouth. He followed the trickle up the hill. That sweet sound—it was like bells.

The sound led him farther up the hills, and the grass grew a mote greener there. The trickle was to his left, and he followed the sound of it ever onward. He jogged, then he walked, then he slowed to a shamble. At last, he fell to the ground in a crawl, and he followed the trickle on his hands and knees until the sound was under him.

It was right below him now. He could hear it, smell it, He could even almost taste it. The air closest to the ground was just the tiniest degree cooler. Tarlos pulled at the grass and dug at the dirt with his chewed fingernails.

The water was there, and the sound was sweet. His dry tongue flopped in his mouth as he took scoop after scoop of dirt from the ground, closer and closer to the water.

Perhaps eight inches into the earth, Tarlos stopped digging. He could hear the water just beneath. It could not be much farther.

He dug in another place just right of the first hole. He yanked at the grass and clawed at the dirt. He dug ten inches, and the ground was dry.

He dug a third time. Dry.

A fourth and a fifth. Both dry.

All the while the sound and smell of water surrounded him, and Tarlos's temples pounded, his mouth was numb, and his head spun.

Now what, came the voice of Krastos.

"Be quiet, you're dead," Tarlos tried to say, but the words came from his parched mouth garbled and incomprehensible.

There was no water here. Tarlos rolled onto his back and looked up at the split peak above him. The white rock face of the mountain was tinted pink in the late afternoon. He grimaced at it, then looked west to the sun. It was a few hours ~~yet~~ until dusk, and it was the hottest part of the day.

"Damn you, Shar," he meant to say, but he did not understand his own slurred speech.

"And why do you say that?" asked a voice.

Tarlos's heart was already exhausted, and the voice made it leap in his chest. He closed his eyes and gasped at the sudden rush of adrenaline. He was dehydrated, probably dying, and the gods had made him hear the voice of a young boy before he died. He could not guess why.

"Are you asleep?" asked the voice. It was a boy, a very young one. Perhaps ten years old, not yet an adolescent. "Can you hear me?"

Tarlos opened his eyes and forced them to roll to the left where the voice came from. The hazy shape of a small person appeared beside him, and Tarlos blinked a few times.

"Who are you?" he rasped.

"Father never gave us names," said the boy. "At least none we wanted to keep." He was naked but for a white tunic around his waist. "Everyone just calls us the twins. Are you thirsty?"

Tarlos nodded. The boy reached into a small pocket in his tunic and took a silver cup from it, the size of a cedar nut. He dipped it in the empty hole Tarlos had dug, and Tarlos groaned.

"Wuh…"

"Here you go." The boy gave the small cup to Tarlos, taking care not to spill it.

Tarlos narrowed his eyes at the cup and then at the boy.

"Do you want it or not? You think getting water is easy? Here." The boy pressed the cup to Tarlos's lips, and Tarlos's eyes widened as he tasted cool, clear water.

He took the cup from the boy and tipped it back. Water, cool, ~~and~~ fresh and clean, gushed into his mouth and down his throat. His shriveled tongue soaked it in, the sores on his cheeks and on his gums screamed. Tarlos ignored the pain. It was hard to give it notice over the heavenly feeling of water in his throat and gut.

After several long seconds of drinking, Tarlos brought the little silver cup away from his mouth to breathe. He looked into it and saw that it was half-empty.

"Is this magic?" he asked the boy. His voice was a broken whisper, but at least he could enunciate again.

"It's water," the boy answered. "What did you say before?"

Tarlos took another long drink, and he relished in the ecstasy of quenched thirst. "When?"

"Before. You cursed the sun. Why?"

Tarlos shrugged. "He never did anything good for me, I guess." He handed the cup back to the boy, and it disappeared back into the little pocket.

"Have you met him?" the boy asked.

"Shar? No. I don't plan to, either."

"He never wanted to meet us," said the boy, "even though we guard his precious gate." He smiled at Tarlos, and the smile was strange and half-given.

"Who else is here?" Tarlos asked. "Your parents? Where do you live?"

"It's just my sister and me. Father left us."

Tarlos scanned the area. There were no signs of a camp or provisions for living. "Has he been gone long?"

"I think it might be coming up on ten thousand years, now. But I really don't keep count."

Tarlos straightened in his sitting position and took a better look at the boy. The water was working through his body now, and his head was clearing. Sitting in front of him, Tarlos saw a boy that was average in almost every way. He was no older than twelve, wearing a common loose tunic. His hair was black, curly, cropped short to his head. There was no dirt on his face or hands, although he was barefoot and sat in the dirt.

Before Tarlos was rehydrated, he had not noticed that the boy's eyes were entirely black with no whites. They were dark like obsidian, empty like the night sky, and if there was any light within them the light was sad.

"You're a jinn," said Tarlos. "A child of Ablis."

"Yes, my sister and me." The boy smiled again, but the darkness stayed in his eyes. "She's up at the gate. I should be, as well. Would you like to meet her?"

"The gate," Tarlos said. "You mean Shar-shu-ka? The way to…the other side?"

"The Scorpion Gate." The boy nodded. "Of course. Come, I'll show you. Can't go through it, of course. Only Shar and Moresh do that. But you can look just the same."

The boy stood and gestured for Tarlos to follow. As Tarlos stood, his knees and spine crackled. The boy led him the rest of the way up the foothills until they came to a sheer rock face that was the start of Shar's Mountain.

"This way." The boy walked around a large outcropping of rock, and behind it was a narrow path that wound upward until it disappeared behind the other side of the mountain.

Tarlos followed. The boy was small and thin, and he jogged without effort through the narrow rock canyon. Tarlos struggled in the tighter places. He sucked in his breath and squeezed between the walls.

The path ended at the top of the mountain, almost at the split peak. It opened up into a small green clearing, bordered on one side by a large flat wall of tan rock. It was more than a half-hour hike, and Tarlos sat down to rest.

"Are you thirsty?" the boy asked. "I only ask because we hardly ever do. Get thirsty, I mean."

Tarlos nodded. In truth, he was fine without another drink, but he had no idea when he would again be able to fill his water bags, and he doubted the boy would give him the magic silver cedar nut to keep.

The boy knelt in the grass, which Tarlos ventured to call a proper green, and he dug a small hole in the dirt with his hand. He dipped the tiny cup in and handed it to Tarlos. Again, Tarlos stared at the cup, and he did not believe that it held so much water within a few visible drops. He was grateful for the water, and he took a long drink.

He gave the cup back and said, "Was that a gift from your father?"

The boy almost laughed. He opened his mouth into a splitting grin as he hid the silver cup away in his white tunic. His teeth were small and sharp, and there were dozens of them. "Father never did anything to us except give us to Shar to guard the gate. No, we have our own power. What little we were born with, anyway."

Four short trees grew in the small clearing, and the trees were covered in broad green leaves. Tarlos guessed that there must be water beneath the ground for the trees and grass to grow so hearty. He wanted that tiny silver cup.

The boy shouted into the trees, "We have a visitor!"

The leaves rustled on the branches, and a small pale girl the same size and apparent age as the boy dropped down to a low branch. She hung there, upside down, her legs hanging onto the tree. Her arms fell down over her head, and her black hair fell longer still. She regarded Tarlos with curiosity and dropped down to the ground with a flip. She landed soft on her small feet and stood beside her brother.

"Who is it?" she asked her brother, but she stared at Tarlos. Her voice was hardly a whisper, and her brother lowered his own voice as he spoke to her.

"He came from the desert," he said. "I haven't asked what his name is."

"What is your name?" the girl asked. Her eyes were as black and solemn as her brother's.

Tarlos hesitated before answering. "My name is Tarlos."

"Why are you here?" asked the girl. "Why have you travelled so far over miles of desert? Tell me."

Tarlos's neck stiffened and he pulled his head back. "None of your business, jinn."

The boy scratched his chin and mumbled to himself. "Tarlos." He turned to his sister. "Does that name sound familiar to you?"

The girl nodded. "Tarlos, son of Ninsun?"

Tarlos drew back at the sound of his mother's name. "How did you—"

"Oh, we know all about your family back in Kesh," said the boy. Both he and his sister were smiling now. "Your mother Ninsun…sorry about that, by the way. She was a wonderful queen and a lovely woman. So, we've heard on the wind."

"And your brother," said the girl, and she stepped closer to Tarlos. Tarlos wrinkled his nose and leaned away. "Krastos, was it? Oh yes, we know all about him." She giggled, and Tarlos felt the bile in his stomach rise.

"Sorry about him, too," the boy said. "I wish I could say I know how you feel, to lose a sibling. But we're both immortal, and we don't know any of our father's other children."

Tarlos did not respond. He had no desire to speak of his mother or his brother to anyone, much less these jinn. He pointed to the split peak.

"How do I get up there?" he asked.

The jinn followed his finger and looked at the peak.

"Why would you want to go up there?" asked the boy.

"I need to get through. To the other side."

"Why? Are you dead?"

"No."

"Are you a god?"

"No."

"Then you can't." The boy shrugged in an apologizing manner. "Rules are rules."

"Are you trying to rescue your mother and brother?" the girl asked. "That's very chivalrous of you, but I'm afraid it doesn't work like that."

Tarlos shook his head. "I'm going for myself, and not for the dead country, but for what lies beyond."

"The Ageless," whispered the boy. He held his sister's hand and sneered. "You're looking for the Ageless! Trying to figure out how they got eternal life and see if you can't do the same. I can save you the trip. You can't."

The boy laughed, and the girl joined him. They shook as they laughed, and Tarlos had to look away. The sound was painful and sick in his ears. They were not children, he reminded himself. They were demons, an intelligent spirit of lower ranked angels.

Children of Ablis, the Discarded One. Half-siblings to the monster that killed his mother and brother.

Tarlos said, "My business is not your concern, jinn. I'm going through that mountain, with or without your permission."

"Oh no," said the boy, and he wiped a tear from his obsidian eye. "It's not a question of whether you have our permission or not. You simply *can't* go through the mountain."

"I don't care about the rules."

"I didn't say *may not*. I said *cannot*. Do you see that peak?" The boy pointed.

Tarlos nodded.

"What comes out of that peak every morning?"

Tarlos lifted his hands in a half-shrug. "The sun, of course. Shar, father of gods."

"And how long does it take for him to climb through the earth every night?"

"It depends on the season, but this time of year I'd say about eight hours."

The boy nodded, and his sister held onto her brother's arm and giggled. The sound sent a clammy shiver up Tarlos's back and neck.

"If it takes the father of gods eight hours to make the journey, how long do you think it would take you, son of Man, before he finds you in his passage and burns you to something less than ash?" The boy lifted one eyebrow and smirked. "You'd have to be able to fly to have a chance of making it."

Tarlos smiled back at him. "But I can fly."

The smirk left the boy's face, and the girl stopped giggling. "I suppose that would make sense," he mumbled. "You are the son of Lakaeus, after all." He shook his head. "I still don't understand what you could possibly have to gain by crossing the dead country. There's nothing useful for you there. Why don't you just go home? Back to Kesh, your kingdom, your people. I'm sure they miss you. Don't you have any children? A wife?"

Tarlos swallowed, and he felt heat rise through his throat. "Are you going to show me the way through the mountain or not? I've wasted enough time as it is. Maybe I should be going."

"No!" the girl screamed, still clinging to her brother's arm. She looked at her brother and said, "This man is driven by despair. He's exhausted and burnt by the desert. Look at him. He can barely stand. He's been so brave to have come this far. We have to help him."

The boy nodded in agreement. "I've never seen such a desperate man. You're dedicated to your goal, then, Tarlos? To cross the dead country and find the Ageless?"

Tarlos gave a single nod.

"And you know that they probably can't help you with your problem? Whatever your problem is."

"That's for me to find out," said Tarlos. "Where is the way?"

The boy sighed and turned around. The girl lowered her head at Tarlos and stared at him through her long black hair. She turned with her brother, and they faced the sheer tan rock wall that bordered one side of the small clearing. The jinn raised their hands to the wall, and the sunlight shimmered over it.

Tarlos blinked, sure that as the wall began to ripple it was the hot sun playing tricks on his mind. The desert wall warped and moved in tiny waves, and the tan color of the rock lightened to a bone white to match the rest of the mountain. Small spindles of black line crawled around the wall as if drawn by some invisible hand. They began at the ground and curved upward several feet above their heads. When the drawing was finished, two scorpions faced each other on the wall with their pincers locked together.

Where the black lines were drawn, the rock began to dissolve, and the rock became steam. It boiled away wherever there was black, and soon the wall had been carved and cut away in chunks and fissures, leaving three-dimensional likenesses of the scorpions. Between the scorpions' pincers, between their legs and stinging tails, the wall had melted away into holes. Behind them, the mountain was hollow and dark.

Tarlos stared in amazement at the gate that had materialized before him, and the two jinn turned away from the gate to face him. They both wore malicious grins, their teeth sharp ~~and several~~, their faces drained and exhausted.

"Rabu-zorak," Tarlos whispered. The Scorpion Gate. He had grown up hearing tales of this far away magical gate that led to the dead country.

The boy and girl spoke together in one voice, and Tarlos squirmed at the sound of them.

"The tunnel leads down into darkness," they said. "All will be black behind and before you and to both sides. You have eight hours to reach the other side. If you do not emerge from the tunnel before Shar enters it in the morning, his fire will engulf you, and there is no refuge from that. May the tunnel of the sun lead you safely to the end of the living world."

The jinn ceased their speech and stepped aside. Between them was the gate, and the stone scorpions vibrated. With a loud *CRACK*, the two scorpions separated from each other at the pincers. They folded outward, and Tarlos stepped back to give them room to open.

Behind him to the west, the sun's last rays were cast onto the desert in lone orange and pink fingers, and Tarlos could almost feel the eyes of Shar on him, daring him to venture into his mountain and see what awaited him.

Tarlos stared into the abyss, and he saw no light at the end of the tunnel.

The boy said, "I wouldn't waste any time if I were you."

Tarlos ran.

CHAPTER TWO

The Dead Country

When Tarlos set out on his journey, he began forming an idea of how long it might be too pass through Shar's Mountain to the dead country. This is why he did not fly at all as he crossed the desert. Flying cost him almost the same amount of energy as running, though it was his mind that became tired instead of his body. He guessed that the tunnel through the mountain would be a fair distance, but he was wrong.

He thought about Shar's path through the sky, and he thought about the dead country. Surely the dead had sunlight for the same amount of time as the living, as the night is roughly the same length as the day in the living world. So then how far could the tunnel possibly be, if the sun travels the same speed through the sky, not slowing or speeding up, and both the lands of the living and dead have the same length of days? The tunnel must be short, for as soon as a day on one side ends, the day on the other side begins.

But then, what if he was wrong, and a day in the dead country was shorter than in the living world for several hours? Or time was irrelevant on the other side?

Tarlos cast the thought aside, knowing that it did not matter, and he held onto his confidence. He was ready for the task ahead, and he knew he would make it to the other side before it was too late.

As he ran into the tunnel, he heard the Scorpion Gate close behind him with a heavy thud, and as the holes in the rock between the scorpions melted back into solid rock, the light in the tunnel faded. Tarlos was not prepared for the darkness. That has overcome him.

This is what it's like to be blind.
He inched forward with his hands outstretched. There was no light at all, and the darkness was thick like tar. This worried him. If the tunnel was short, he should be able to see light on the other end, the light coming from the dead country. But there was no light, and Tarlos could see absolutely nothing. He walked, and he kept his hands in front of him.

Twice, he found himself walking into the wall on the right side, and he adjusted his course. A few times he waved his hands above his head to guard against low ceilings, but there were none. This made sense; the sun was enormous, and the tunnel must be large enough for it to fit.

He was comforted by this realization, and he thought that if the tunnel was large enough to fit the sun, it was large enough for him to fly if he was careful. Slowly, slowly, he lifted himself into the air, and he remembered that great feeling of weightlessness that he had not experienced since before Krastos died. He could not see the walls or floor of the tunnel, so he could not be sure how high he was. He missed that feeling.

It was always a secret pride he kept within himself, knowing how birds and dragons felt to soar hundreds of thousands 0f feet from the ground, seeing huge cities as tiny dots and great forests as green splotches in the red desert sands. In this tunnel, though, there was no such feeling. As far as he could tell, he was floating in empty space with nothing above or below him.

He propelled himself forward, and he kept his hands in front of him all the while. He tried to keep his flight slow, yet faster than he could run, while still being safe from slamming into the rock walls. There was no way to tell how fast he was flying, as there were no landmarks to be seen. The air moving past his ears and waving through his hair was enough to tell him he was advancing quickly enough.

There was no way to measure time. After what felt to Tarlos like several hours, he began to worry. What if he had seriously miscalculated, and the sun would rise through the tunnel at any moment? There was still no light to be seen at the end, so he could not be close. And yet he knew he had been flying for some time. He pressed on harder and faster, feeling the air whip past him rougher than before.

Hours later, or at least what felt like hours, Tarlos felt weary. He did not know that he was slowly nearing the floor of the tunnel until his feet grazed the smooth rock. He flinched at the touch of it, and he realized he had been drifting off to sleep.

Tarlos slapped himself across the face. The sound echoed loudly through the tunnel, bouncing back and forth a thousand times before dissipating.

"Get up," he told himself, and his voice joined the echoes.

He lifted himself a few inches from the ground and then felt that part of his mind give out like a pulled muscle. Tarlos cried out in pain and crumpled to the ground. His temples throbbed, and he pressed the heels of his hands against them, rocking back and forth on his knees.

Trying again, he hovered for a moment. He barely cleared the ground before the feeling of a hot knife piercing his head as ~~and~~ he screamed in agony. Once more he fell down.

No more flying, then.
He stood, still pressing his hands against his temples, and swallowed. His mouth was dry. He went to grab for his water bags and felt that they were not there. After a moment's panic, he remembered that he had left them in the clearing with the jinn, and they were empty anyway. They would have only slowed him down. But he needed water. He rammed a fist against his forehead and squeezed his eyes shut.

Tarlos took a few steps forward. His legs were painfully sore, although he had not used them for several hours. He jogged on. No more flying. Only feet from here on out.

He had no idea how much time he had left, and so he ran. He kept one arm outstretched ahead of him, the other hand pumped beside him to help his legs push faster and longer.

He guessed he had run for about half an hour before his heart made a funny rushing feeling, and he paused to catch his breath. The salty Sweat poured down his forehead and into his eyes, burning them. Dripping further down his arms, back, and torso. He bent down, placed his hands on his knees, and puked. Perhaps running so fast for so long without water was not such a good idea after all.

The sun would be rising any time, now. He had to move no matter how much it hurt.

He tried to run, but he had stitches on both sides of his belly, and his throat was raw, and his dry nose stung as he breathed. So he walked, but he kept a brisk pace, and he always kept a hand out in front of him.

Tarlos felt the wind on his face and in his hair. He rubbed his sweaty face, feeling the breeze cool him, and he thought how amazing it felt to fly again. He stopped, remembering that he had been walking for a long time now. He should not be feeling the wind on his face.

But the wind was there. It was faint, but he could feel it on his sweaty forehead, and the ends of his hair flickered.

Tarlos lifted his hands in front of his face. It was too dark to see. He brought them closer until they were no more than half an inch in front of his eyes. Unless he was imagining it, he could almost see the faint blurry shapes of his hands. That meant there was light, however small of an amount there was. He was almost there.

He ran, ignoring his screaming sides and burning throat and lungs. Yes, there was a breeze, and it was picking up.

Farther and farther. *Follow the breeze.*

He ran for a mile before he noticed that he no longer needed to stretch his arm ahead of him. He could see the ground. The light was becoming stronger with the breeze.

A flicker of light twinkled ahead. His breath caught, and he paused to stare down the tunnel. He moved his head from side to side, and the tiny speck of light seemed to blink on and off.

He forced himself on. The end was in sight, and a stiff breeze blew across his face. He closed his eyes and smiled at it, loving the feeling of that fresh air. The light grew brighter, and before he reached the end of the tunnel he had to shield his eyes from its intensity.

The tiny prick of light grew into a tunnel opening as large as the sun, and Tarlos found the energy within himself to sprint.

The tunnel opened up to a mountain face, and the mountain was almost a mirror image of Shar's Mountain on the other side. Just below the tunnel opening, foothills covered in lush green grass rolled away from the mountain. Tarlos reached the opening of the tunnel and collapsed. He rolled down the grassy hill, not bothering to slow himself until he had come to a full stop at the bottom.

Tarlos panted and swallowed as he lay in the green grass, and he stared upward into the evening sky.

I'm here. The dead country.
He reminded himself that no living man had ever reached this place since the creation of mankind, and he took pride in that fact.

Trees with green and yellow leaves surrounded him and lined the foothills that led to the mountain. They shimmered and shook in the breeze, and Tarlos rubbed his face as the wind cooled his burning, sweaty skin. Above him, the sun was setting.

Shar, the sun god in his fiery chariot, soared over Tarlos and dipped down toward the mountain. The fire of the sun was bright and burning, and Tarlos turned away to save his eyes. When the light in front of his eyelids faded, he opened them and looked at the mountain above him. The tunnel opening glowed, and then the glowing faded to black. Shar had moved on, and soon the living world would see the sun once more.

Tarlos did not know what the dead country would look like, but he had imagined something grimmer than what stretched out before him. He had imagined grey skies, cold wind, sprinkling rain that never let up and never quite became a full shower. He thought the landscape would be painted in tones of brown and grey, and that the sun and stars would always be hidden behind an overcast sky. There would be souls wandering around the place, not having anywhere to go, but desperate to get there anyway.

None of this turned out to be true. There was more life in the dead country than in the desert Tarlos had crossed. A lush green forest began at the mountain slopes and flushed down into a great valley, which was green from horizon to horizon. Although he could see no birds, he could hear them chirping in the distance and in the trees. There were no animals that he could see, but if there were birds then there were certainly other creatures in the forest.

From his vantage point halfway up the mountain, Tarlos saw over the tops of trees and all the way to the edge of the valley. There the mountains fell into flatlands and disappeared into the distance. With the sun gone through the mountain to the living world, the sky was falling into gloomy darkness. Tarlos squinted down into the valley, and his eyes adjusted to the fading light. On the far horizon to the east, Moresh was rising. She was almost at full face, and Tarlos was grateful for that.

Down in the valley, perhaps two miles away from the mountain and nested in the foothills, a light flickered through the trees. Tarlos peered through the forest, widening his eyes as much as he could against the dark. There was a white light, and a faint line of smoke floated upward from it to disappear into the sky.

Tarlos made his way down the mountain. The slick rock on the mountain's face became gravel and grass and then dirt as the trees grew thicker around him.

The birds had stopped singing, and Tarlos assumed it was because they were sleeping.

Do the dead sleep?
Tarlos tossed the question around in his mind for a few moments and then cast it aside.

Ahead, the sound of rushing water was growing apparent. Tarlos's pace quickened, and he batted away low-hanging branches and kicked at the waist-high ferns and conifers. The moon was bright, and Tarlos found that it was easier to see at night in the dead country than it was in the living world.

The sound of water was a few feet away when Tarlos stopped. Whatever water he was hearing could only be one thing. He would have to see it to confirm his theory.

It was a river, and the rapids it made were in a small stretch of it. The water bubbled up over rocks, creating small eddies and white foam. The river was about twenty feet across, and to the left and right Tarlos could see that it was much deeper than in this section.

At the sight of the water, which appeared to be fresh and clean, and at the feel of the cool mist on his face, Tarlos felt his thirst more than ever. He wanted nothing more than to plunge his sunburned head into the river and drink long and deep.

But it would kill me. This is the Styx. This is the river Ilshu uses to ferry the dead to his country.
The water was tempting, and Tarlos licked his dry and cracked lips as he stared into it and listened to it bubble over the rocks. He held himself back. He had not come all this way to kill himself in the Styx.

The white light he saw while on the mountain was on the opposite shore, just beyond the tree line. Tarlos could see the clear outline of a building through the trees, and smoke rising from its chimney. He looked up and down the river, searching for a bridge. If there was one, it was not close by.

Keeping the river on his right, he walked upstream. He would not get lost as long as he stayed within sight of the Styx.

To his left, in the forest, a cricket chirped. Tarlos paused and turned to the sound. The cricket chirped again, and Tarlos raised a corner of his mouth in a half-hearted smile. He had heard nothing but birds since arriving in the dead country, and he did not know how long it had been before then that he had heard anything but the calls of vultures. He entered the forest, and he kept his eye on the river. The cricket chirped again.

A tree with round green leaves stretched high into the night sky, and the stars shone through its branches. At the base of the tree was a boulder, flat on the sides and the top. Tarlos crouched beside it and saw a small green cricket sitting there. Its tiny antennae wiggled at the sight of him, and the cricket chirped again.

"Are you alone?" Tarlos whispered.

The cricket sprang away, disappearing into the undergrowth. Tarlos frowned and shrugged. Now he knew that there really was life here, and that was something he would never have imagined.

He moved to stand and caught sight of something on the boulder. There were marks on it, carved, and the marks were strange letters that Tarlos did not recognize. But although he did not know the foreign writing, he could read it.

John Talbot was here.
Tarlos's eyes narrowed, and he ran his hand over the carved sentence. A cricket chirped behind him, and he stood and turned. The river rushed before him, and the moonlight glinted in the water. A small footbridge, only a few feet wide, stretched from the near shore to the far shore. Tarlos was sure it was not there a moment ago. The cricket was nowhere to be seen.

He walked across the bridge, listening to the Styx rush away beneath. On the other shore, Tarlos stepped off the bridge and looked around. A small sign sat to his right, sunk into the ground on a long post. He stepped closer to read it. There were two words:

Windmill District

CHAPTER THREE

Tavern and Boat

The building sat at the edge of the trees several yards from the riverbank. It was wooden, two stories, with a few windows in the front, ~~and~~ a wood porch, and steps leading up to the door. Orange light from a fire glowed through the windows on the first floor, and shadows crossed on the inside. Hanging above the door was a sign written with more strange letters that Tarlos did not know, and yet he could understand them.

Tavern

Tarlos looked around. There was no one around the building. He found himself standing on a dirt path, wide enough for a cart to pass over, and the path led up and down the river. Upstream, Tarlos could just make out the dark shapes of more buildings in the dark, within the cover of trees. They were smaller than the tavern, and smoke rose from a few of their chimneys. The ones without smoke had no light in the windows.

He climbed the steps and approached the door. The handle was strange to him. It was not a brass handle, as were all the door handles in Kesh. This one was round and brown, shiny with use, sticking directly from the wood like a growth. He touched it. It was cool and hard. Metal. He grasped it, feeling the cool metal in his palm, and he tried to move it down; that was how all door handles in Kesh worked. But this one did not slide down. He bit his lip and twisted the round handle instead, and it gave way with no hesitation. There was a click, and the door swung inwards with a low and slow creak.

The smell hit him first. Most of it was smoke from the fire that bellowed in the fireplace at the wall. Above the fire was a rack with garments hanging over it, dripping dry. There was the sour smell of alcohol in the air, though it was like no alcohol he had smelled before. This was a more bitter smell than the mead and beer he was used to in Kesh. But the smell of drink reminded him of his dry throat, and his thirst returned stronger than ever.

And then there was the smell of cooking food. A counter near the back of the tavern was covered in dirty plates, and there were leftover bits of food on them. There was a door behind the counter that swung freely on a hinge, and more smells drifted from whatever room was behind it. Meat, vegetables, bread, and fruit were the smells that Tarlos recognized. There were more smells, but he had no labels in his mind for them.

The tavern was one big room, and more than a dozen tables were littered around the place. Tarlos guessed that on a busy night, this tavern could hold more than a hundred people. Tonight, however, there were only a few. One man sat in a far corner, farthest from the counter, with a wide-brimmed hat that sat low on his head, shading his face. He was drinking something amber-colored from a large clear cup. Another man and woman sat at a table in the center of the room, and they seemed to be enjoying a plate of meat with what appeared to be small carrots and brown sauce. Tarlos's mouth watered at the sight and smell of it.

A woman stood behind the counter, rubbing a transparent cup with a small towel. She was the only one who looked up at Tarlos as he entered the tavern.

"Welcome," she said, waving the hand that held the towel. She jerked her head to the side. "Come on, have a seat."

Tarlos said nothing as he stepped toward the counter, weaving between the tables. None of the other people looked at him as he passed.

He sat on a cushioned stool and placed his arms on the counter. He looked at the woman and wondered what part of Edorath she came from. Her hair was brown and thick, and it fell in waves over her shoulders. Her nose was small and freckled, and her dark brown eyes were lined with dark eyelashes. Her lips were full, and her face was round and childlike. She was not as tall as Tarlos, but he felt that she carried with her an air of authority regardless of her size or gender.

"Hungry?" she asked. She set the cup and towel to the side and smiled at Tarlos.

He nodded. "More thirsty than hungry. What is that?" He pointed at the strange cup.

She glanced at it. "What?"

"That…cup."

"What do you mean, what is it?"

"What's it made out of?"

She raised an eyebrow as she smiled and flicked the cup with her finger. It gave a small delicate ring, and Tarlos leaned back in surprise.

"They don't have glass where you come from, huh?" she said. "You want some water? You look like you need it."

Tarlos nodded, and the woman held the glass cup under a small metal pipe. She twisted a knob on top, and water gushed into the cup. She handed it to him, and he drank slowly. The water was delicious.

When the cup was half-empty, he paused and stared at it. "Where does this water come from?"

"The spring, a few miles away. Why?"

He shrugged. "Just making sure." But he knew that if the water had come from the Styx, he would be dead already. He gave the empty glass cup back and asked for another, and the woman gave him one without a word.

"Hungry?" she asked again.

"Yes, I'd like some meat. Do you have boar?"

She laughed, and the laugh was sweet and friendly. It made Tarlos smile, although he was also confused about why she laughed at all.

"How about a burger?" she asked him, then disappeared behind the swinging door.

Tarlos did not know what a burger was, but he waited patiently for it as he sipped at his second cup of water. He chanced a glance behind him at the others. The man was still drinking alone in the corner, and the couple was still eating their meal.

The woman came back a few minutes later with a white plate. She set it on the counter in front of Tarlos, and Tarlos stared at the thing she had brought him.

"What is this?" he asked. He poked the top. It felt like bread, but it was wrinkled and covered in small seed-things. He could plainly see that there was some kind of meat between the bread, but the other things that were there he was not sure about.

"They don't have burgers there, either?" she replied. She shook her head. "Man, where *did* you come from? Or I guess the better question would be *when?*"

Tarlos raised an eyebrow. "I don't understand." He picked up the bread on top of the pile and smelled it. There was yellow and red slime on the other side, and he grimaced at it.

"It's just ketchup and mustard. I hope that's okay." The woman turned to grab another dirty cup and began cleaning it with her small towel. "Who doesn't like ketchup and mustard on their burger? I guess someone who's never had one. Don't eat it like that! Here…" She set her cup and towel down and slid the plate over to her side of the counter. "You don't mind cooties, do you?"

Tarlos did not know what a koo-dee was, so he shook his head. The woman grabbed the burger in her hands, keeping the slices of bread on each side of the innards. She brought it to her mouth.

"Like this." She mimed biting and chewing, then gave the burger back to Tarlos.

He grabbed it as she had and brought it to his mouth. It seemed too thick to fit, but he opened his jaws wide and did his best. He bit down, feeling the soft crunch of the green vegetable and the hot juice of the meat, which he guessed was beef. There were other tastes he could not identify, but they blended well, and he chewed and swallowed. His stomach roared with hunger.

"Good, huh?" the woman asked. "Better than McDonald's, anyway." She went back to cleaning her cups.

Tarlos nodded, having no idea what she was talking about. He ate his burger in silence. He had no idea how hungry he was until he tasted this food, and he realized he had not eaten anything in several days. Perhaps more than a decan.

The woman set the glass cup on a shelf beside her which held dozens of others. She smiled at Tarlos and narrowed her eyes a bit as she inspected him.

"Are you okay?" she asked.

Tarlos almost laughed. Instead, he returned her smile and shook his head. "No, I'm not okay. Not yet."

She nodded. "You look…well, you don't look good. Usually when people come here, they look refreshed and sort of…refurbished. Know what I mean?"

"Yes." He did not know what refurbished meant, but he understood her point. His cheeks were hollow. His face was frost-chilled from the cold nights and sunburned from the hot days, and his arms were thin and tired. And of course, there was the depression. He had carried it with him since Krastos died, and it sat heavily on his shoulders and made him slouch. He knew he must have been a sight to the woman.

He finished his burger, and the woman took the plate away to the back room. When she returned, she reached beneath the counter and brought up a green glass bottle. She used a special metal tool to pop the lid off, and she gave it to Tarlos.

"I think you need a beer," she said.

Beer was something Tarlos knew. He drank with eagerness. After a few gulps, he took the bottle from his mouth and looked at it. He smacked his lips.

"This isn't like any beer I've had before."

The woman asked, "Is there a lot of beer where you come from?"

"We invented it."

He drained the bottle, and the woman gave him another. Before she could take the lid off with the metal tool, Tarlos raised a hand. "Please, I'm already very tired."

She smirked and put a hand on her waist. "It's not like you can get drunk or anything. Go on, it's free. In life I'd never turn down a free drink."

Tarlos nodded and took a sip from the second beer. He cracked his neck, which was painfully sore, and he rolled his shoulders to try and relax his muscles. All at once his body remembered how exhausted it was, and Tarlos let out a heavy sigh.

He took the tooth from his pocket and held it in his open palm. It hovered a few inches above his hand and spun slowly in the air for a few moments before dropping.

The woman stared. "That's some trick."

"It's not a trick. I'm a Holder."

The woman seemed not to hear that. She looked at the tooth with fascination, and she did not blink. "Where did you get that?" she asked. She ran a finger through her thick brown hair, pushing a loose strand behind her ear.

"I found it in the desert."

"When?"

"A few days ago, I guess. Maybe a decan. Why?"

She shrugged, still staring at the tooth. "It looks familiar."

"Teeth do look similar."

"I guess. What's a decan?"

"Ten days," he said, and then asked, "What's your name?"

She looked up from the tooth and into Tarlos's eyes. "You're new here," she said. "You have a lot to learn. Wait a minute…" As Tarlos put the tooth back in his pocket, the woman put a hand on the side of her face and her eyes grew wide. "How do you have that with you? You don't get to bring anything with you. That's impossible."

Tarlos licked his lips and took another sip of beer. "Listen," he said. "This is going to be strange to you, but you should know."

The woman nodded. "I know."

"Know what?"

She gave Tarlos a friendly smile and patted his hand on the counter. "It's not easy for anyone. You come down here, you have no idea where you are or who you are, no idea how you got here. It gets easier with time. Eventually your memories come back and you get to remember your life. But not your name. That's lost forever. Maybe it makes it easier knowing we all had to go through it at some point."

Tarlos looked down at the woman's hand. It reminded him of another hand he liked to hold in the privacy of his room back in Kesh. He pulled his hand away. "Well, that's just it. See, I'm not dead."

The woman stepped back and made a short noise through her nose that sounded like a laugh. "That doesn't…" She shook her head. "I mean, it usually takes a few days to know that you *are* dead and that this is purgatory. It's common not to believe you're dead at first, but…how did you know what I was talking about in the first place?"

Tarlos squeezed the glass bottle in his hands. It was cold in his dry cracked palms, and perspiration ran down the neck of the bottle. "Because I know where I am. I've never heard the word *purgatory* before, but I know what this is. I know you're dead, and they're dead." He threw a finger behind him, indicating those who were eating and drinking at the tables. "But I'm not dead. And if I can help it, I never will be."

The lock of hair behind the woman's ear came loose once more and she pushed it behind her ear again. "I got some bad news for you. You are dead. No one thinks so at first. That's normal, so don't feel bad. You get used to it. Really, being dead isn't all that different from being alive. We still have the same food, and the company isn't bad. Don't believe me? What's your name, then? Can't remember, can you? None of us can. That's part of being dead."

"My name is Tarlos."

The color fell from the woman's face, and she held her tongue between her teeth. She took a step back.

Tarlos continued, "My father was Lakaeus and my mother was Ninsun, king and queen of Kesh. My twin brother was Krastos. They're all dead. I'm not."

The woman said nothing for several seconds. Her eyes were wide and white, and her lips were pressed together in a thin line. She did not step closer to Tarlos. "If that's true, how did you get here?"

"I went through Shar's Mountain."

"Where is that?"

"At the edge of the desert, where the sun rises. It opens up not far from here. Haven't you seen it?"

She shook her head, and the hair behind her ear fell again. "I grew up in Oregon. Newport. There was definitely no desert there. Not on that side of the state, anyway."

It was Tarlos's turn to look confused, and he leaned back a bit in his stool. "Where is Org-en?"

She came back to the counter and to Tarlos, and she placed a hand on his. She gave it two soft pats and said, "I know this is a lot to take in. It's better to just accept it. I don't know how you remember your name and the names of your family members, but…" She looked around the tavern, at the people eating and drinking and speaking in low tones. "Trust me, it'll all make sense eventually."

"I'm not dead," Tarlos said. "I'll never die."

"Oh? How's that?"

"On the far side of this country, at the end of the Styx, is the Ageless country. I will find the Ageless and discover their secret to immortality."

She nodded. "Well, I've never heard of anyone who lived forever. Except gods. I guess if that's what you feel like would be the best thing…" She shook her head and sighed. "I can't imagine that, though. Living forever. I had a good, full life. I honestly feel satisfied and rested now."

Tarlos took another drink. "If you had been what I've been through, you would say different."

The woman laughed. She threw her head back and let out three huge guffaws. She ran a ran over her face and through her long brown hair.

"I could tell you stories from my life," she said. "Not to discredit what horrible things you've no doubt been through—I'm not saying your life hasn't sucked—but I had myself a doozy. More pain and heartbreak than anyone should ever have to go through."

Tarlos nodded in understanding.

"But," she continued, holding up a finger, "I would never want to live forever. Even if it meant I could right all the wrongs that happened in my life."

Tarlos said, "I don't think you understand, then. Have you ever actually known someone who died? Have you seen their dead husk and tried to shake them awake, knowing they will never breathe again or speak your name?"

The woman stared at him, unblinking, unsmiling. Her eyes glazed over as if her memories were flashing over her face in a slideshow, and none were pleasant. She said nothing to Tarlos, but she nodded.

Tarlos sighed. "And yet you say you would not want to right those wrongs or live forever."

"Tarlos…" She turned away for a moment, picked up another glass cup and began cleaning it. "People are born. They live, they die. That's just the way of things. Until the end comes, you should just enjoy your life. Sure, mourn those you lose, but don't lose your own life over them. Eat good food, take hot bubble baths, dance and sing and love…" She inspected the cup in her hands and nodded. "That's what you should be doing."

She set the cup down. "I wish I had done more of that, honestly. It's funny, when it's all over, what you really regret is not doing more of the little things."

Tarlos asked, "What are you trying to say?" His voice came out louder than intended, and the woman drew back in surprise. "My heart is *sick* for those I've loved, who are gone forever! What you say, it means nothing. I'm going to the Ageless country, and I *will* find the way to immortality. And I will never die as my mother and brother did."

The few others in the tavern had turned their heads to Tarlos as he spoke, and when he finished he could feel their eyes on him, and he lowered his head. The people turned away and continued their conversations and drinks and meals.

The woman scratched her ear and raised an eyebrow at Tarlos. "Do what you need to do. A person's goals are important, no matter how misconstrued they are."

Tarlos turned his head and scanned the three people in the tavern, then looked back to the woman. "Is there anyone here who can take me down the river? I've travelled a long way, and I'm exhausted. I'd rather take the trip by boat than hike the rest of the way down the riverside. I have no idea how much farther I have to go."

"You're going to the very end of the river?"

"Yes, to the Ageless country. On the other side of this country, at the end of the Styx."

She turned her head to look at him sidelong. "You sure you're not from Greece?"

"I don't know what that is."

She nodded and took up her cleaning again. She threw a nod to the side, toward the man drinking out of a mug alone in the corner. "That guy has a boat. He trades up and down the river with the other communities. He knows he doesn't have to, because we all have everything we need, but I guess it gives him something to do. I think it reminds him of his life. Maybe he can take you where you need to go, although I've never heard of that place. But maybe he has."

"What's his name?"

She let out a chuckle. "Very funny."

Tarlos moved to stand up from his seat. The woman grabbed him by the wrist before he could go.

"Woah, woah," she said. "You trynna leave tonight?"

"As soon as possible." He tugged his arm free from her grip.

She smiled with sympathy. "I can promise you he won't want to leave tonight. People around here tend to sleep at night. You told me yourself you're exhausted. There's a spare bedroom upstairs with a shower. Get a good night's sleep and talk to him in the morning."

Tarlos considered this for a moment. "He'll be here?"

"Oh yeah," she said with a nod. "He's here every day for all three meals, and sometimes more often than that, unless he's on the river. Here." She reached below the counter and brought out a key, handed it to Tarlos. It was the smallest key he had ever seen, half the length of his finger, and it was thin and light and silver. "Take a shower and get some sleep. I know you need it."

Tarlos took the key and nodded. "Fine. This is your tavern, so I'll respect your wish."

She patted his hand one more time. Her eyes were deep with memory and experience, and the freckles on her nose stood out as she blushed. Why she blushed, Tarlos had no idea. "I just work here," she said. "Goodnight, Tarlos."

Tarlos climbed the steps to the second floor and found the empty bedroom at the end of the hallway. There was a large bed with thick blankets, a dresser, and a table with a single chair. A door led somewhere in the back of the room, and Tarlos opened it. He recognized the huge white oval bowl to be a tub, although it was much smaller than he was used to. There was a pipe hanging over it, much like the one the woman used to give him a cup of water, and the knobs on the pipe looked similar. He guessed they worked the same way.

He twisted the knobs as he had seen the woman do, and water gushed from the pipe. Tarlos put his hands beneath it, then withdrew them in surprise. The water was hot, straight from the pipe. A small lever sat on the pipe, and he moved it back. The water stopped coming from the pipe and instead came from above, turned into a thousand drops of rain through a piece of metal with several holes.

"Must be the 'shower'," Tarlos said to himself. Feeling the warmth of the water, he stripped his clothes off and climbed into the bath. He ran his hands through his matted hair, combing it with his fingers. Not seeing any soap, he scrubbed himself with his hands as best he could. The water became thick and muddy, and it spiraled down the drain. His neck and nose pained in the water, having been sunburned worse than the rest of his body. After it was too late, he wondered if this water came from the same spring the woman had spoken about, or if it came from the river. But if it was from the Styx, he would be dead already.

He twisted the knobs the other way, and the water stopped its flow. He squeezed the water from his hair as best he could. Hanging on the rack on the wall was a blue towel, and he used it to pat himself dry. The towel was warm and soft, softer than any towel he had ever used.

A sort of fold-up knife sat on a basin beside the bath, and he picked it up and tested the edge with his thumb. It was razor-sharp. He ran a hand across his cheeks and chin, feeling the stubble that was growing too long. He used the knife to shave, and he had no more stubble.

The bed beckoned to him, and he climbed into the clean fluffy sheets. The mattress was more comfortable than any bed he had slept on in his life, and the pillow was a cloud beneath his head. He was asleep in less than a minute.

Tarlos woke to the smell of food cooking. He pulled his dirty shirt on, and his filthy trousers, then laced up his sandals. His hair had been damp when he got in bed, and now it stood out in every direction. He wet it in the bathroom and tamed it as best he could, wetting his face while he was there to wake himself up.

Downstairs, the tavern was filled with dozens of people. They all spoke loudly and excitedly, laughing and moving from table to table, sharing food and drink. Tarlos stopped at the bottom of the stairs to observe them, and he wondered how many people lived in this community. At a glance, he guessed there were at least a hundred people here this morning.

"Tarlos!" called a familiar voice. "Good morning! How'd you sleep?"

Tarlos held up a hand in greeting to the woman behind the counter. She was dealing out plates of steaming food, and the smell made Tarlos's mouth water and stomach grumble. On the counter, there were plates of bread and boiled eggs, and stacks of what looked like thin bread. There were pitchers of juice and coffee and tea and milk. Tarlos never imagined that there would be such things in the dead country.

"Hungry?" asked the woman. She waved him over, and Tarlos approached the counter. A man with short brown hair and a long nose smiled at Tarlos and moved aside for him.

"Heard you're the new guy," said the man. His eyes were green. Tarlos had never seen green eyes.

"I'm just passing through," Tarlos said.

"That's what she tells me." The man clapped Tarlos on the back, and Tarlos's eyebrows knit together. "Well, I gotta get back," the man said. "I hope we get to officially meet soon." He nodded at Tarlos, and Tarlos gave him a weak smile in return. The man grinned at the woman and said, "Later." He left them, disappearing through the crowd.

"Who's that?" Tarlos asked the woman.

"Oh, just a friend from before," she said. "So, what'll it be? Eggs? Bacon? Pancakes? French toast?"

"Um…" Tarlos scanned the plates with the food, recognizing only a few dishes. "What do you like best?"

"Waffles. But we don't have any today, sorry. I'd recommend French toast and raspberry syrup." She made him a plate and poured him a cup of dark coffee. The cup was not glass; it was white and—Tarlos guessed—made of clay, like the cups in Kesh.

"Cream, sugar?" she asked.

Tarlos shook his head, not understanding what she meant, and the woman pushed the plate across the counter to him and handed him an eating utensil. He held it in his fist and gave the woman a questioning look.

"Man, you really are from the Bronze Age," she said. "It's a fork. You use it to eat with, so you don't get your hands messy. Like this." She took another fork and pretended to eat with it. "I'd really like to know about your homeland and your life. When you have the time to talk."

Tarlos choked down the French toast. It was entirely too sweet for breakfast food, but he did not wish to be rude. He finished his plate before moving to the coffee, when it was cool enough to drink.

"Is that man here?" he asked.

"The boatman? I think so." The woman stood on her toes and craned her neck to see over the crowd. "Yep, I see him. He's at his usual table. Looks like he chose pancakes today. He always chooses biscuits and gravy when we have it."

Tarlos thanked the woman for the food, and she took his plate and cup away.

The tavern was crowded, with at least four people to each table, all of them speaking and eating. The place was filled with the sound of utensils on plates, beverages being poured, conversation mixed with laughter. The only table that was not full was in the corner of the tavern, and the boatman sat there alone, poking at his food.

Tarlos navigated his way through the tables, avoiding the chairs that were pushed too far from their tables, making narrow gaps between them for Tarlos to squeeze through. Hardly anyone looked up at him, and those who did gave him a friendly smile.

The man who ate alone was wearing a brown hat with a wide brim, and thick-soled boots made of leather. His shirt was plain blue and buttoned down the front, and his trousers were tan and worn at the knees. He bent over his food, the wide brim of his hat covering his face. Tarlos approached slowly, and he cleared his throat when he reached the table.

The man raised his head, and Tarlos was met with pale blue eyes. Tarlos had seen blue eyes only once before, and something painful tried to rear its head in his mind. He pushed it away. There was stubble on the man's cheeks and chin. His mustache was thick and long, curled up at the ends. He nodded a greeting at Tarlos.

"Have a seat, if you want," he said with a gruff voice. Tarlos took the seat across from him, and the man continued poking at his pancakes and eggs.

"I hear you have a boat," said Tarlos.

The man raised his head once more and pushed his plate away. "I hate eggs. Don't care much for pancakes, neither. I always get biscuits and gravy when I can, but this ain't heaven yet. Yeah, I got a boat. Why?"

"I need to get down the river." Tarlos folded his hands together on the table.

The man sucked his teeth. "Mm-hm. Nothin down there."

"Have you ever been?"

The boatman shook his head. "No, but I been far enough, I guess. Far enough to see that there's no point in going any further."

"I need to get to the end of the river. I have business in the country on the other side of this one.

"You ain't got no business anywhere but here, son," the man grumbled. He picked up a cup of coffee and drank half of it. He sighed and licked his lips, then ran a finger across the handlebars of his mustache. "This is where the good Lord sent you, and you'd do best to accept it and continue your existence in peace. Ain't no use dreaming about what else is out there. You're dead. What's else to know?"

"I'm not dead."

The man smirked. "That's what we all think at first. There's no shame in it if you're new here. But it's best to accept it as quick as you can. If you put it off too long, it gets real difficult to let it sink in later. And it always sinks in."

"My name is Tarlos," he said with a stern face. "I came to this country through Shar's Mountain, I'm not dead, and I need to get down that river."

The man raised his eyebrows. For a while, he said nothing. He stared at Tarlos from the shadow of his hat's brim, studying him. After several moments, the man said in a softer voice, "Way is dangerous. The river isn't meant to be floated down by the likes of us. It's for the Reaper, only."

"I understand that you float it regardless."

The man nodded. "Yeah, well, I never was one for keeping the rules. They say the water is poison, but that's never been a concern for me. Might be for you, though."

"It might."

The man stuck his little finger into his mouth and picked something from his teeth, then flicked it away. He looked past Tarlos, into the crowd, and his eyes stayed fixed to something for a moment. Before Tarlos could turn to see what the man was staring at, the boatman spoke.

"You say your name's Tarlos. Are you sure about that? It's no name I've ever heard before."

Tarlos nodded. "Tarlos, son of Lakaeus, king of Kesh."

The man looked back to whatever he was staring at, and this time Tarlos turned to follow the man's gaze. A small woman with olive skin and black hair, and almond-shaped eyes like those who lived in the Southern Isles, stood reverently at the counter, speaking to the tavern woman. Tarlos looked back to the boatman and saw that he was still staring at the small woman.

"Did you know her when you were alive?" Tarlos asked.

The boatman snapped his gaze back to Tarlos and cleared his throat. He finished his coffee and slammed the empty cup down on the table. He cleared his throat and wiped his mustache.

"Listen," he said, "I've been down the river once, not all the way but further than anyone else, I think. I told myself I'd never go again. But…" His eyes flicked up one more time to the counter. The man sighed.

"What?" Tarlos said.

"I never heard of Kesh. And I never met someone here who remembered their name, neither, but it seems like you're telling the truth." He cracked his knuckles, and his knee began to bounce beneath the table. "What the hell, I'm dead anyway. Let's go before I change my mind."

The boat was long, slender, and flat. A box sat on top large enough for them to stand up in, with a bunk and a chair and a wash basin. Ropes and posts were strewn about the deck, ready to be put to use if there was anything to ship up or down the river.

"Hardly ever go down," the boatman told Tarlos as he untied the mooring line from a small wooden post on shore. He gave the boat a shove out into the water, then jumped aboard as the boat floated away. "Hardly anyone in that direction, anyway. I mostly go upriver. Pain in the ass, really. Gotta push against the current with a pole, and it does get mighty tiring after a while. I always thought that after I died I wouldn't feel tired anymore. I guess that's what I get for being philosophical. Should be fun, though, for the most part. At least I ain't alone this time."

The man sat beside the rudder and steered the boat downstream. Tarlos took a seat on the deck and leaned against the wall of the box-room. He played with the tooth in his pocket.

"So, Tarlos," said the man. "I never heard that name before, and I been everywhere, or pretty much everywhere. America, Australia, New Zealand, Japan, even as far as India in my early years. Where are you from?"

Tarlos took the tooth from his pocket and held it in his palm. "I've never heard of any of those places. I'm from Kesh, in the Fertile Valley."

"Never heard of that, neither. Is it nice there?"

"I suppose."

The tooth floated a few inches above Tarlos's hand and flipped around two or three times before settling back down again. He closed his fist over it and sighed.

"What on Earth?" said the man. He let go of the rudder for a moment to take a step toward Tarlos. He lifted his chin and stared down at Tarlos's closed fist. The rudder turned slightly, and the boat jerked. He went back to steady it. "Was that thing just floating?"

Tarlos nodded. "I'm a Holder."

"A what? Did you make that move?"

Tarlos lifted his eyebrows. "You don't know what a Holder is?"

The boatman shook his head. "Enlighten me."

Tarlos took a moment to organize his thoughts, then spoke with reverence. "I've been able to do it since I was twelve. I inherited it from my father, and he got it from his mother, on and on since the first people. The firstborn always inherits the Power."

"Okay," the man said. He tipped his hat back and scratched his forehead. "I guess I've seen stranger things."

"There are four Powers," Tarlos said. He spoke softly now, not really caring whether the man was listening or not. "Space, Creatures, Mind, and Time. But the Power of Mind has been lost since—"

"What does the time power do?" the boatman interrupted.

Tarlos glanced at him and shrugged. "Control time. Speed it up, slow it down. But I don't think they can make it run backwards."

"Hang on," snapped the man. "You're telling me there are people from your world who can slow time." It was more of a statement than a question.

"Yes."

"I'll be damned," he mumbled. "I knew a bunch of people who could do that."

"Do what?" Tarlos mumbled. His eyes closed as he leaned back against the wall.

"Slow time. On my honor, I knew em."

Tarlos opened his eyes. The boatman was grinning, staring off across to the south shore, mindlessly steering the boat at the rudder, bobbing it up and down in the water.

Tarlos said, "You lie."

The man took his eyes from the shore and looked at Tarlos. His smile diminished a bit, the ends of his mustache coming down. "Excuse me?"

"You could not have known people who could slow time. There is only one in each generation. Perhaps you could have known two, a parent and a child, or even also a grandparent. How many did you know?"

"Dozens," the man said. "They were called samurai. They had this thing inside them they called chi, and they used it to slow down or pause time for as long as their strength would let them. I remember there was this one samurai, older than dirt, who could stop time for days, or longer, I don't know. He used it to meditate for hours and hours without losing a second in the real world, and he'd read every book ever written, I'm sure. The man knew more than was good for anyone. Hey, can I see that?" He pointed at Tarlos's pocket.

"The tooth?"

"Yeah."

Tarlos handed it to him, and the boatman held the tooth close to his squinting eyes. His tongue darted between his lips.

"I swear I seen this before," he said with a low voice. "Or at least something just like it." He gave it back. "Pretty, though."

"Strange," said Tarlos. "The woman at the tavern said the same thing."

The boat floated along the Styx quietly and smoothly. The man talked and Tarlos listened. At least, he pretended to listen. Most of the time Tarlos was sure that the man spoke only to hear the sound of his own voice, and that he did not care whether Tarlos listened or not.

It must be lonely for him, floating the river all the time by himself. He's his only entertainment.

The man had packed dried meat, bread, and water. There were boxes of fizzy drinks, which the tavern woman gave Tarlos before they left. He did not care much for the bubbly flavored water, as it was too sweet, and the bubbles hurt his throat and his nose. The boatman had one every hour or so and belched his approval whenever he finished one. By the fourth day, half the boxes of the drinks were gone.

The first time the man threw an emptied drink cup—which was made from a very thin metal that the boatman called "sodakan"—overboard into the water, Tarlos watched it land in the Styx and begin to melt. It sizzled and boiled, and the metal merged with the water around it and mixed with the Styx, dissolved forever.

"Why doesn't the boat dissolve?" Tarlos asked.

"Nothing makes sense here," the boatman replied.

"What would happen if we touched it?"

The man shrugged as he cracked open another drink. "We'd die, probably."

"But you're already dead."

The boatman swallowed, belched, smacked his lips. "There's dead, and there's dead, and there's dead."

At the end of the fifth day, as the sun set on the dead country, Tarlos realized that he had not heard the boatman's voice in well over an hour. This was strange to him, and he opened his mouth to ask if everything was all right. But the boatman caught his gaze before Tarlos could speak, and he raised a quick finger to his lips.

"You'll wanna be quiet," the man whispered, so softly that Tarlos almost did not hear him.

Tarlos mouthed the word *why*, and the man pointed downstream. The sky was growing dark, and Tarlos had to strain to see where the man was pointing. But the moon was at full face and in view, and the landscape was still shrouded in black and getting blacker. Tarlos moved to ask the man why it was so dark when he saw that the light of the moon and the stars stopped above the water ahead of them, just above the level of their heads. An invisible bubble covered the Styx and its shores, not allowing in any natural light. On the left shore, Tarlos could make out trees and rocks in the fading light. On the right, he stared into the face of nothingness. Only the faint outline of a building could be seen through the veiled darkness.

The boat came closer as they made their way down the river, and the building enveloped in darkness neared. Tarlos could now see how large the building was. It was the size of the stone temple in Kesh, or bigger. This building was also made of stone, and the back of it merged with a rocky hill behind, giving the impression that the building continued on underground for an unknown distance. Tarlos could almost make out the thick green vines crawling up and clinging to the walls.

The boatman once again held a finger to his lips and held the rudder steady. Tarlos's breath was caught in his chest, and he made no sound as they passed.

And then he heard it. He thought it was a wounded animal crying out for help but only signaling predators of an easy meal. But the more he listened, the more it was apparent that it was no animal.

It was the sound of moaning. It was the sound of weeping. It was the sound of intense emotional and psychological pain. It was the sound a mother makes when her child is killed, the sound a child makes when his father does not return home from war, the sound a man would make if he could look back on his life and see all the missed opportunities that would have made his life a happy one, the sound of being shown all the hurt you caused and the people who suffered because of your selfishness. It was the sound of anguish that would never end, and those who wailed knew that it would never end.

Tarlos felt his eyes water. The sound stank in his ears and was sour in his mind. He looked at the boatman, who held fast to the rudder, and the boatman wiped a tear from his cheek. Tarlos said nothing to him until the boat had floated well past the dark bubble and the building was invisible behind a bend in the Styx. The weeping and groaning faded, and Tarlos sighed in relief. His breath was shaky, like the breath of one who had been crying for several minutes.

The boatman mumbled, "That's why I never come this way. I guess if there's a Hell, that's it. It's some wonder I didn't end up there, and you better believe I thank God every day that I didn't."

"I think I've heard of that place," said Tarlos. "Although I never really put much effort into imagining what it looked like. And I suppose a part of me never believed it existed at all. The High Priestess in Kesh called it the House of Dust. I think…" He swallowed a lump in his throat. "I think that's where my father is. And it'll probably be where I end up if I don't find the Ageless."

The boatman raised an eyebrow at him. "How'd you figure?"

Tarlos shrugged with one shoulder. "It's a long story."

"Well, we got a ways to go, yet. I'm up for hearing a long story if you're up for telling one."

Tarlos sat for several minutes in silence, and the boatman did not press him to speak. At length, Tarlos nodded and took a seat in his usual place against the wall of the room. After another moment's consideration, he reached for a fizzing beverage and cracked it open using the tab on the top of the strange metal cup. He began:

"I suppose I should first explain that when my father, Lakaeus, was still a prince, he wasn't permitted to marry until his father, king Hestos, was dead…"

CHAPTER FOUR

Back Again

The sun was setting on the dead country, and soon Shar would enter the tunnel in the mountain to rise in the east of the living world. The air was still and warm, and the brightest stars had already begun to poke through the purple sky. The Styx was steady, gurgling over rocks at its banks, and insects buzzed at its surface.

Tarlos took a deep breath of air that seemed so fresh despite belonging to the dead. He smiled as his lungs filled, then he let it out slowly. This might be the last time he would be in this place, and he wanted to savor the feeling. Some distance away was Shar's mountain, and the sun was nearing the gate.

The bald man stood beside Tarlos. He wore a grey hooded shirt with a large pocket on the belly, which he kept his hands in. The hood was up over his bald head, and as he faced west the red light of the setting sun illuminated his kind features. He watched Tarlos enjoying his last breaths of the dead country and smiled.

"Are you sure about this?" he asked Tarlos.

Tarlos nodded. "I just have to do one thing. Right a wrong. And then…" He shrugged. "Whatever happens, happens."

The man nodded and patted Tarlos on the back. "Best of luck to you. I don't think we'll be seeing each other again, but in the grand scheme of eternity I guess anything is possible."

Tarlos shook the man's hand, and the man's grip was firm and warm.

"Goodbye," Tarlos said. "And thank you."

With a blast of air, Tarlos launched himself into the sky toward the mountain. The bald man watched from the ground, using a hand to shield his eyes against the sunlight. A small green cricket pounced on his shoulder and chirped.

The man said to the cricket, "I'm glad I got to help someone one last time," and the cricket chirped once more before jumping off the shoulder and into the foliage to the side. The man waved to Tarlos, knowing Tarlos could not see him, and then he turned back to the village.

The sun had entered the tunnel a few minutes before Tarlos neared it, and he slowed down to give the sun a head start. As the sky darkened and the stars came into full bloom, Tarlos counted to one thousand before he decided that he had waited long enough, and he flew through the hole in the mountainside.

This time it was not so dark. He kept pace with the sun, leaving a thousand feet or so between it and himself. The sun lit the tunnel with a red and yellow glow, and Tarlos saw for the first time just how mind-numbingly enormous the cave was. Even with the light, Tarlos could hardly see the stone ceiling above him, and it was just as spacious to the left and right.

But he had no time to appreciate the magnitude of the sun or its tunnel. He focused, speeding on through the mountain with the sun just ahead, and he did not count how many seconds passed before the sun squeezed through the other side.

A cool morning breeze brushed Tarlos's face as the sun rose into the sky and the Scorpion Gate opened before him. Only moments after the sun passed through, the gate began to materialize back into the mountain, and Tarlos pushed harder to make it through in time.

The morning air of the living world slapped him to attention, and the shock made him stumble and drift to the ground. He took a moment to catch his breath and give his mind a rest.

"Hey!" called a voice.

Tarlos turned and saw a young boy with black eyes and black hair standing beside him. He was not there a moment ago.

"Hello again," said Tarlos. "Remember me?"

"You can't just *leave*," said the boy. He grimaced, annoyed and angry.

"I promise I'm coming back. I just have to do something first."

"You had your whole life to do something," cooed a different voice, and Tarlos looked up to see the girl hanging upside down from a tree branch. "No second chances."

"Sorry." Tarlos raised himself a few feet into the air. The children screamed painful screams, and Tarlos drew back farther into the sky.

Below him, the jinn twins twisted into sick caricatures of their young and innocent selves. Their mouths grew wide, splitting their faces across the middle. Their small white teeth rusted to a dark red and grew and stretched into sharp fangs. Their brows protruded over their black eyes and their hair receded back to reveal wrinkled scalps, and their scalps were covered in sores and dark spots. Their arms grew long, and their fingers became claws, and they reached upward toward Tarlos as he put more and more distance between him and the demons.

The jinn spoke in unison, and their voices were the wailings of Hell. The words were screeches and growls, and Tarlos did not understand what they said. The jinn tried to reach him as they stood as high as they could on their long-extended legs and stretched clawed arms.

It was their job to keep anyone from going into or coming out of the dead country, and Tarlos understood that. The jinn twins were frightening and disgusting, but Tarlos held no ill will against them.

"I promise I'm coming back," he shouted down to them from his vantage point. "Today, tomorrow, someday. But I will come back."

The demons cried as Tarlos flew west, and they shrank back to their common forms of young children. The girl lowered her head in defeat and sat beside her climbing tree. She brought her bended knees to her chin and rested her hands on them. The boy kicked a rock, and it skidded along the yellow grass and landed in a bare patch of dirt.

"What will he do to us?" asked the girl.

The boy followed Tarlos with his black eyes and licked his lips. "I have a feeling we won't have to worry about him anymore."

The desert was a blur beneath him.

Wind in his hair, on his face, stinging his eyes.

How long had it been since he had flown like this? In the open air, the ground as far below him as the sun was above?

After a while the sound of the wind faded into the background of his mind, and to him the world was silent. Peaceful.

He would return to the dead country. But first, one last thing.

Kesh was a small circle, a red coin surrounded by yellow sand. Tarlos positioned himself above it and enjoyed the sight of his kingdom. He studied the brickwork of the walls, the ancient roads, the stone temple that reached so high. He saw the fields of grain and corn just beyond the wall, and the lush garden beside his cedarwood palace. This would probably be the last time he would see Kesh, and he took his time.

Gently, slowly, he lowered to the city, and the walls and buildings came up to meet him. He stopped as he became level with the top-most floor of the cedar palace, where the royal apartments were. The shutters were closed, and the curtains did not move in the calm noon air.

Tarlos did not speak with his mouth, but thought loudly, *Ablis.*

The curtains drew back, pulled by an invisible hand. The shutters opened, slamming against the walls inside. A child cried. Tarlos swallowed.

The being who called himself king floated out of the window, sneering at the real Tarlos as he came closer. His hair floated in the air as if underwater, and in his eyes was a burning of annoyance, ~~and~~ anger, and hate.

"I can't believe," said Ablis, "that you would be this stupid." His voice was no longer the cloned voice of Tarlos. It was the sound of rocks grinding together in an avalanche, the sound of lightning cracking over a storming ocean, the sound of a tornado in an empty plain.

"I need to finish this," Tarlos told him. His voice did not shake or tremble. He was past the point of fear or worry.

"You're dead already," Ablis howled, "so I won't harm you. I will destroy you. Your spirit will not return to the dead country, nor will it suffer in the House of Dust. I will wipe every memory of you from your family and the world, blot your name from every record, and I will make it a sin to even utter your name, and soon there will come a day when Tarlos son of Lakaeus might as well have never existed in the first place. Then you will truly be dead."

Tarlos did not respond, and he turned to the wall behind the great garden in the courtyard and flew. Ablis followed behind him, shouting curses in languages Tarlos did not understand.

Tarlos led Ablis over the wall and to the small area where he had died. He landed there in a small crater of sand, and the sand erupted over him in a plume. His body was nowhere to be found. At least Ablis had the decency to keep it from being scavenged by birds and desert wolves. Nearby was the patch of cacti, and Tarlos ran to it.

"There is no use in running," Ablis said behind him, and Tarlos turned to meet the hellish voice. Ablis grabbed Tarlos by the throat and squeezed. Tarlos tried to cough or wheeze, but no air was allowed to escape. "Tell me, before I destroy all memory of you," said the god, as his face rippled and his eyes blazed. "What did you hope to gain by coming back?" He loosened his grip just enough to allow Tarlos to answer.

Tarlos took a swallow of air and coughed. "Needed…to…fix…what I…did," he panted.

Ablis smiled, and his teeth were sharp. "I am eternal. You cannot kill me."

"Maybe not," Tarlos said. He held up his hand, and wrapped around his fingers was the necklace, and the tooth dangled in front of Ablis's face. "But I can get rid of you." Then in his mind, he thought as loud as he could.

OLD ONE!

Something pulled behind his stomach, and Ablis's eyes widened in horror. The god tried to pry his grip from Tarlos, but an unseen force kept them glued together. There was that too-familiar slurp sound, and the two were pulled upward and inward through the dimensions. The physical universe turned inside out and back again, folding in on itself and unfolding into the next dimension, over and over, and all the while Ablis screamed in horror. Tarlos brought both hands to the hand on his throat and pulled. The fingers came loose, and he and Ablis were separated.

"*NO!*" Ablis cried.

Tarlos pushed at the Discarded One, and Ablis drifted away into an unknown dimension. He cried out at himself and to the other gods, to his parents Shar and Moresh, but they were far beyond that now, and no god heard his pleas. As the multiverse became a series of small marbles around them, Ablis floated away between them, and the multiverse became one again. Ablis was gone—a being lost in the void of voids, the space between spaces, the collective of universes, the tide and current of the Continuum.

Orange.

The smell of burnt almonds.

Hello again

"It's done," Tarlos said. "I did what I meant to do. Ablis can no longer harm my world or my family or my kingdom."

Is that what you wanted

"If I hadn't left in the first place to fulfill a selfish desire, none of this would have happened. I'm satisfied."

Good
Now what

If Tarlos had a face, he would have knit his brow in confusion. "I'm dead, aren't I? Aren't you going to send me back to the dead country?"

If that is what you wish
But you have also earned your immortality
Will you not take that?

"I…" Tarlos searched for the right words to explain his change in perspective. But surely this god of gods understood. Knowing the thoughts of Tarlos's heart and mind would be effortless.

So Tarlos said instead, "Kesh needs a king. Katla needs a husband. Gilmesh needs a father. Send me back to Kesh. Let me live the life I should have been living all along, and when the time comes I will embrace death." Tarlos smiled to himself, although he had no mouth. "Life is beautiful and fleeting, and it is beautiful because it is fleeting."

So be it.

"Tarlos!"

He felt a few light slaps on his cheek, and he opened his eyes. He lay on the sand, where he had died, staring up into the blue cloudless sky.

"Oh, thank the gods, he's okay!"

A series of gasps sounded all around him, and Tarlos lifted his chin to his chest. There was a group of people surrounding him, including half a dozen guards, several slaves, and Katla holding Gilmesh. Lugal stood over him, his face inches from Tarlos's.

"That was some hit you took," Lugal said. "Try to sit up."

He helped Tarlos to sit on his backside, and he gave Tarlos a bag of water to drink.

"What happened?" Tarlos asked, then took a drink. It was delicious.

"We saw you fight with Ablis," Lugal said. "We thought he was going to gut you with that spear, and there was nothing we could do about it." He wiped his sweaty forehead and laughed. "But I guess he changed his mind and left. We ran out to get you as soon as he was gone. You've been out for a few minutes."

Tarlos felt at his belly where the spear had gone through before he died and felt nothing. He was clean and rested.

"How long have I been gone?" he asked Lugal.

"What do you mean? You mean the three years you disappeared?"

"No, just now, I..." *I died. No...The Old One must have taken me back to that day.* "Never mind."
"Can you stand?"

Tarlos nodded. Lugal helped him to his feet, and Tarlos took another drink of water.

The group parted, and Katla stood there with her young son in her white arms, and Tarlos stared at her. After a few silent moments, Tarlos approached her and looked at Gilmesh. He was sucking on his fingers.

"I hope," Tarlos told Katla, "that in time you'll be able to forgive me for leaving you."

A single tear fell down Katla's cheek, and she smiled at Tarlos. She handed Gilmesh to him, and he held him awkwardly at first. Gilmesh wiggled uncomfortably and wiped his wet hand on Tarlos's face before finding a comfortable position, and then he laid his head on Tarlos's chest. Tarlos felt a lump in his throat as he held his son for the first time, and he looked up to see everyone looking at the two of them with approval and happiness.

"Welcome home," said Katla.

CHAPTER FIVE

Epilogue

Gilmesh climbed a tree. It was one of the largest trees in the Gardens of Kesh, and he tried to reach the top before he was called in for dinner. His father the king watched him below.

"Almost there!" Gilmesh shouted down.

He heard his father shout back, "I can see you! You're so tiny up there! Be careful!"

The last branch that would let him see through the top-most leaves had always been just out of reach. But this had been a good summer for him. Gilmesh was now twelve, and he had grown several inches over the last six months. The growing pains were painful sometimes, but he endured in excitement for the coming of his Power. This would be the year that it would surface within him.

He reached for the last branch, trying not to look down at the dizzying drop below.

"Are you there?" he called down to his father.

"I'm with you until the end," king Tarlos replied. As he spoke, Gilmesh felt imaginary arms supporting him, but not helping him to climb. Gilmesh was thankful for the safety net, but he wanted to defeat this tree on his own.

Trusting his father, Gilmesh jumped from the branch he stood on and grabbed hold of the branch above. Now that he was holding onto the highest branch, he saw that it was no more than a few inches from the one he had stood on since he was small, always afraid to take that last step. It was almost anticlimactic.

He pulled himself up and sat on the branch. His head came through the leaves on top, and he beamed down at his father. King Tarlos laughed and clapped his hands. Gilmesh felt the invisible hands wrap around his waist and brace him beneath the arms, and king Tarlos lowered his son to the ground.

"Did you see me? Did you see me?" Gilmesh shouted. He hugged his father, who grinned with pride.

"I barely could, you were so high!" Tarlos knelt to be eye-level with his son. The boy grinned with excitement, and in his squinting brown eyes Tarlos caught a glimpse of his own brother.

"Gilmesh!" came the frightened voice of his mother. He turned to her, standing in the stone archway that led into the palace. "What did I tell you about climbing that tree?"

"I was here, Katla," the king said in a reassuring tone. "You know I'd never let him drop."

Katla placed one hand on her hip and the other on her round protruding belly. "Would it be too much to ask to not have you raise all our children to be like you and Krastos?"

"You say that like it would be a curse." Tarlos smiled.

Katla smiled back and waved. "Come on. Time to eat. You can climb more tomorrow." She waited for Gilmesh to run to her, and he hugged her as he did his father.

"You should've seen me!" he said. "It was so high, Father said he could barely see me!"

Katla placed a hand on her son's back and led him inside, and all the while Gilmesh babbled on about his great accomplishment.

Tarlos stayed back for a moment. He looked up at the tall tree and the way the orange sunset filtered through the leaves. He admired a small cricket that jumped across the lilies and orchids that surrounded the tree.

Do you think it was worth it? Krastos asked.
Tarlos looked from the cricket and the tree to his pregnant wife and son. Both were smiling, and he knew both were happy. So was he.

"Yes," he said. "It was worth it."

9 781728 891729